COLLECTED POEMS

COLLECTED POEMS

EDGAR ALLAN POE

INTRODUCTION BY KEVIN J. HAYES

BARNES & NOBLE

NEW YORK

Introduction and Suggested Reading
© 2008 by Barnes & Noble, Inc.

Edgar Allan Poe's poetry was published from 1827 through his
death in 1849. Some works were first published posthumously.

This 2008 edition published by Barnes & Noble, Inc.

Cover art: *Raven* (gouache on paper); Private Collection;
© Look and Learn / The Bridgeman Art Library International

ISBN-13: 978-1-4351-0930-8

Printed and bound in the United States of America

1 3 5 7 9 10 8 6 4 2

Contents

INTRODUCTION

TO READ THE POETRY OF EDGAR ALLAN POE IS TO ENTER THE mind of a genius, a dreamer, a madman, a lover. Readers often associate Poe with the macabre, but his verse captures many different moods. Sometimes he expresses despair at the loss of a loved one. Other times he voices the uncertainty of a man teetering on the brink of sanity. Elsewhere he is an idealist seeking the realm of pure imagination. Throughout his poetry, he lifts readers from the everyday world to place them in a dream-like state, a wonderful realm where the rules of normal behavior no longer apply.

Poe's life, by contrast, was filled with disappointment, frustration, poverty, and sadness. The son of actors David and Elizabeth Arnold Poe, Edgar was born in Boston on January 19, 1809. Before he turned three, his father had abandoned the family, and his mother had died from tuberculosis. Her plight became known to Richmond theater-goers, including John and Frances Allan, who took Edgar in, educating him to be a gentleman. After Poe's first year at the University of Virginia, Allan pulled him from school and put him in the counting house of Ellis and Allan, his mercantile firm. For an aspiring poet, few positions could be more onerous. The two quarreled bitterly. In 1827,

Poe left Richmond for Boston, returning to his place of birth to remake himself into a poet. Over the next few years, he published his first collection of verse, joined the army, quit the army, moved to Baltimore, published his second collection of verse, dreamed of military glory, entered West Point, left West Point, and published a third collection of verse. Throughout this time, Poe and Allan continued quarreling. Allan died in 1834 a wealthy man but left Poe nothing. To eke out a living, Poe largely abandoned poetry for prose, moving back and forth from Richmond to New York to Philadelphia serving in various editorial capacities. In Richmond on May 16, 1836, he wed his teenaged cousin Virginia Clemm, whose death from tuberculosis eleven years later left Poe distraught. He returned to poetry toward the end of his life, when he created some of his finest lyrics before dying from mysterious, alcohol-related causes in Baltimore at the age of forty.

Tamerlane and Other Poems (1827), Poe's first collection of verse, reveals several literary influences. His debt to the influential English Romantic poet, Lord Byron, is most important, but Poe's early verse was also influenced by the eighteenth-century British playwright Nicholas Rowe, whose *Tamerlane* Poe knew, and an obscure nineteenth-century Baltimore poet, Garrett Barry. The title character of "Tamerlane," the most substantial poem in the collection, bears little resemblance to the real-life Tamerlane, the fourteenth-century ruler of Samarkand. Offering his personal story to a Catholic priest, Poe's Tamerlane relates how he recognized his own genius for leadership, fell in love, and then left his lover to pursue conquest, intending to return home eventually to make her his queen. After conquering much of the world, he returned only to find her dead. Sadly, he realized that the price he had paid for his empire was a broken heart.

In his subsequent verse, Poe would renounce Byron to develop his own unique style. He published *Al Aaraaf, Tamerlane, and Minor Poems* (1829) in Baltimore while awaiting his appointment to the U.S. Military Academy at West Point. This collection contains revised versions of many poems from the earlier one and some new poems as well. In "Al Aaraaf," the book's most significant poem, Poe imagined an ideal world inhabited by angels and enlightened human souls who mediate between heaven and the rest of the universe, conveying an awareness of beauty to the others and thus bringing them closer to God. In terms of both imagery and ideas, "Al Aaraaf" is Poe's most difficult poem. William Wirt, best known for his life of Patrick Henry, was one of Baltimore's most well-respected men of letters. Seeking Wirt's opinion, Poe sent him a manuscript copy of "Al Aaraaf." Wirt recognized its originality but otherwise could make no sense of it. "It will, I know, please modern readers," he told Poe. "I should doubt whether the poem will take with old-fashioned readers like myself." Though "Al Aaraaf" is not entirely successful, its conception of an ideal world where an aesthetic philosophy triumphs over all other base concerns is magnificent.

Admitted to West Point in 1830, Poe wrote much verse there. His satirical lines about the instructors endeared him to his fellow cadets. When he proposed a published collection of verse, they eagerly subscribed, but when the volume appeared, the cadets felt cheated. *Poems* (1831) contained none of the satirical verses that had so endeared them to Poe. By the time *Poems* appeared, however, Poe had left West Point. Dissatisfied with his life there, he quit attending classes, quit going to drill, quit doing pretty much everything the army ordered him to do. He was brought up on charges, court-martialed, and dismissed.

Poems opens with "Letter to Mr—," in which Poe first laid out his aesthetic theory. A seminal document in the critical history of American verse, Poe's preface to *Poems* is also known as the "Letter to B—." It is typically reprinted in collections of his critical essays and is not included in this collection of poetry. Traditionally, literature was supposed to delight and instruct; Poe dared to deny poetry's instructive purpose. Poetry has, he observed, for its "*immediate* object, pleasure, not truth." Approaching a definition of poetry, Poe explained, "Music, when combined with a pleasurable idea, is poetry; music without the idea is simply music; the idea without the music is prose from its very definiteness." Poe's aesthetic theory strongly influenced poets throughout the world. Among twentieth-century American poets, H. D., William Carlos Williams, and Robert Pinsky and others, have expressed gratitude toward Poe's poetic theory and appreciation of his verse. *Poems* contains some fine new lyrics exemplifying his theory, including "Fairy-Land"—Robert Pinsky's favorite Poe poem— "To Helen," and "The City in the Sea."

"To Helen"—H.D.'s favorite Poe poem—is the best of the new ones, but this early version differs from the version of "To Helen" readers have since come to love. The speaker of the poem explains that Helen of Troy has brought him home "To the beauty of fair Greece, / And the grandeur of old Rome." Poe revised and republished "To Helen" several times. In 1843, these lines reached their final form, and Helen brings the speaker of the poem home "To the glory that was Greece, / And the grandeur that was Rome." As these revisions suggest, Poe was a meticulous craftsman. He often republished individual works several times, tinkering with them each time. Poe generally improved his poetry in revision, but he sometimes marred his short stories with too much tinkering.

Poe turned to fiction the same year *Poems* appeared. More than anything, he longed to be a poet, but personal poverty and the demands of the literary marketplace forced him to turn his back on poetry to try his hand at short fiction. In the early 1830s, a number of magazines sponsored literary contests. Some were solely fiction contests. Those that offered premiums for different genres of literature typically valued fiction over verse. To have any hope of making a living as a writer, Poe realized, he had to start writing fiction. He did so with extraordinary results. Poe revolutionized the genre of the short story by bringing a poet's sensibility to the writing of fiction. The aesthetic principles he used in his poetry he applied in his short fiction. For the next decade and a half, fiction would dominate Poe's output, and his verse would take a back seat. To a contest sponsored by a Baltimore magazine in 1834, for example, Poe submitted an entire volume of stories in manuscript but only one poem.

"The Coliseum," the poem he submitted to this contest, shows him continuing to experiment with music and ideas but in a minor key. The blank verse form Poe chose for "The Coliseum" suits its subject matter. The speaker of the poem is a traveler on a secular pilgrimage. He wishes to immerse himself in the realm of ancient Rome to learn what he can. He seeks the "springs of lore" that lie within the Coliseum. Reaching Rome after much weary travel, he takes strength in what the Coliseum represents. His contemplation of these ancient ruins echoes Fingal's contemplation of the ruins of Balclutha, a walled town belonging to the ancient Britons in "Carthon," one of James Macpherson's popular Ossianic poems. Fingal intones, "The thistle shook there its lonely head: the moss whistled to the wind." Poe's traveler observes, "Here, where the dames of Rome their yellow hair / Wav'd to the wind, now wave the reed and thistle!" Poe's traveler gradually shrugs off his melancholy and listens to what the ruins say. The building stone retains memories of what has occurred within the Coliseum. Poe clearly understood how physical objects could serve as repositories of memory and how sensitive, imaginative minds could unlock their memories. "The Coliseum" is a moving articulation of this idea.

Some of the best poems Poe wrote in the coming years he wrote for inclusion in his short stories. "To One in Paradise"— William Carlos Williams' favorite Poe poem—is the composition of the title character of "The Visionary," a romantic tale in which two lovers make a suicide pact in order to unite their souls in a greater love after death. "The Haunted Palace," which forms part of "The Fall of the House of Usher," serves as a microcosm of the story as a whole. Sung by Roderick Usher, "The Haunted Palace" presents a metaphor for the mind that indicates Usher's awareness that he is going mad.

Poe put together enough stories by the mid 1830s to form a book-length collection of tales, but publishers hesitated to accept it because collections of short stories did not sell well. He kept writing for the monthly magazines and Christmas annuals. By the end of the decade, he had written enough short stories to fill two volumes, which he finally published in December 1839 as *Tales of the Grotesque and Arabesque*. This collection constitutes a landmark in literary history, but Poe met its publication wistfully. In a contribution to *Alexander's Weekly Messenger* published the same month *Tales of the Grotesque and Arabesque* appeared, he offered the following conundrum: "Why ought the author of *Grotesque and Arabesque* to be a good writer of verses? Because he's a poet to a *t*. Add *t* to Poe makes it Poet."

Poe made a triumphant return to poetry with the publication of "The Raven" in January 1845. It met with instant acclaim, being reprinted in numerous magazines and newspapers across the nation, memorized by countless readers, and parodied by many nineteenth-century wits. "The Raven" caught the attention of Evert Duyckinck, who edited the prestigious Library of American Books for Wiley and Putnam. Duyckinck soon asked Poe to contribute a collection of verse to the series. *The Raven and Other Poems* appeared that September. This volume included most of the poems from Poe's earlier collections as well as those few he had written since. The book contributed to the popularity of "The Raven" and continued to fuel Poe's literary reputation. Some people even started calling him "Raven."

The poem also prompted Poe to write "The Philosophy of Composition," an essay in which he detailed his creative process using "The Raven" for example. This essay contains Poe's famous pronouncement that the death of a beautiful woman is "the most poetical topic in the world" and that "the lips best suited for such topic are those of a bereaved lover." It is difficult to know precisely how to take this essay. In places it appears genuine but sometimes it seems tongue in cheek. Poe, one of the great geniuses in world literature, denies the idea of genius in the writing of poetry. He makes literary composition seem more like a matter of plugging variables into a formula. Perhaps the best way to test what Poe says in "The Philosophy of Composition" is to use it as a standard against which to measure his subsequent verse.

"Ulalume" (1847), for example, follows "The Raven" in terms of both its subject and its narrative voice—a bereaved lover relating the death of a beautiful woman—but it differs in other respects. In "The Philosophy of Composition," Poe said that he first decided to set "The Raven" outdoors, but concluded that "a close *circumscription of space* is absolutely necessary to the effect of insulated incident: it has the force of a frame to a picture." With "Ulalume," Poe challenged himself to write a poem set in forest and field, achieving a circumscription of space through the use of an overarching canopy of tree branches. "The Philosophy of Composition" must be read as both a statement of poetic principles but also as an author's challenge to surpass his own personal standards.

Each time Poe gathered his poems for a collection, he organized them differently. In *Tamerlane and Other Poems*, for example, he led with the collection's most significant work. In *Poems*, alternately, he gathered his brief lyrics together at the beginning of the collection and placed the longer and more difficult poems at the end. This organization makes *Poems* more approachable than either of his previous collections. Poe's variable organization suggests that there is no set order in which to read the poems and gives us the freedom to read them in whichever order we wish.

Organized in chronological order according to their original composition, the present collection begins with "Tamerlane," but readers need not start there. Feel free to dip into this volume anywhere. Start with an old favorite. Then choose a poem you have never read before. Or open the book at random and read whichever poem appears. There's no need to read every one before rereading a new favorite. Reread a single poem as often as you wish: Poe's verse repays frequent readings with new insights. Reread some of the poems on special occasions. "Ulalume," for example, is the greatest Halloween poem in the English language. And "The Bells" is a good one to read around New Year's Day. Then late one night, when you feel you are ready, curl up in your comfy chair, open up this volume, focus your lamp onto the surface of the page, and put yourself in the ideal world of "Al Aaraaf." Poe's verse brings readers into an imaginative realm where the beautiful holds sway.

Kevin J. Hayes, Professor of English at the University of Central Oklahoma, is the editor of *The Cambridge Companion to Edgar Allan Poe* and author of *Poe and the Printed Word, The Road to Monticello: The Life and Mind of Thomas Jefferson,* and *An American Cycling Odyssey, 1887,* among other books. He has received the Virginia Library History Award presented by the Library of Virginia and the Virginia Center for the Book.

COLLECTED POEMS

TAMERLANE

Kind solace in a dying hour!
　　Such, father, is not (now) my theme—
I will not madly deem that power
　　　　Of Earth may shrive me of the sin
　　　　Unearthly pride hath revell'd in—
　　I have no time to dote or dream:
You call it hope—that fire of fire!
It is but agony of desire:
If I *can* hope—Oh God! I can—
　　　　Its fount is holier—more divine—
I would not call thee fool, old man,
　　But such is not a gift of thine.

Know thou the secret of a spirit
　　Bow'd from its wild pride into shame.
O yearning heart! I did inherit
　　Thy withering portion with the fame,
The searing glory which hath shone
Amid the jewels of my throne,
Halo of Hell! And with a pain
Not Hell shall make me fear again—
O craving heart, for the lost flowers
And sunshine of my summer hours!
The undying voice of that dead time,
With its interminable chime,

Rings, in the spirit of a spell,
Upon thy emptiness—a knell.
I have not always been as now:
The fever'd diadem on my brow
    I claim'd and won usurpingly—
Hath not the same fierce heirdom given
      Rome to the Cæsar—this to me?
        The heritage of a kingly mind,
And a proud spirit which hath striven
      Triumphantly with human kind.

On mountain soil I first drew life:
    The mists of the Taglay have shed
    Nightly their dews upon my head,
And, I believe, the winged strife
And tumult of the headlong air
Have nestled in my very hair.

So late from Heaven—that dew—it fell
    ('Mid dreams of an unholy night)
Upon me with the touch of Hell,
    While the red flashing of the light
From clouds that hung, like banners, o'er,
    Appeared to my half-closing eye
    The pageantry of monarchy,
And the deep trumpet-thunder's roar
    Came hurriedly upon me, telling
      Of human battle, where my voice,
    My own voice, silly child! Was swelling
      (O! How my spirit would rejoice,
And leap within me at the cry)
The battle-cry of Victory!

The rain came down upon my head
    Unshelter'd—and the heavy wind
    Rendered me mad and deaf and blind.
It was but man, I thought, who shed
Laurels upon me: and the rush,
    The torrent of the chilly air
Gurgled within my ear the crush
    Of empires—with the captive's prayer—
The hum of suitors—and the tone
Of flattery round a sovereign's throne.

My passions, from that hapless hour,
    Usurp'd a tyranny which men
Have deem'd, since I have reach'd to power,
      My innate nature—be it so:
    But, father, there liv'd one who, then,
Then—in my boyhood—when their fire
      Burn'd with a still intenser glow
(For passion must, with youth, expire)
    E'en *then* who knew this iron heart
    In woman's weakness had a part.

I have no words—alas! To tell
The loveliness of loving well!
Nor would I now attempt to trace
The more than beauty of a face
Whose lineaments, upon my mind,
Are—shadows on th' unstable wind:
Thus I remember having dwelt
    Some page of early lore upon,
With loitering eye, till I have felt
The letters—with their meaning—melt
    To fantasies—with none.

O, she was worthy of all love!
    Love—as in infancy was mine—
'Twas such as angel minds above
    Might envy; her young heart the shrine
On which my every hope and thought
    Were incense—then a goodly gift,
        For they were childish and upright—
Pure—as her young example taught:
    Why did I leave it, and, adrift,
        Trust to the fire within, for light?

We grew in age—and love—together—
    Roaming the forest, and the wild;
My breast her shield in wintry weather—
    And, when the friendly sunshine smil'd,
And she would mark the opening skies,
I saw no Heaven—but in her eyes.

Young Love's first lesson is—the heart:
    For 'mid that sunshine, and those smiles,
When, from our little cares apart,
    And laughing at her girlish wiles,
I'd throw me on her throbbing breast,
    And pour my spirit out in tears—
There was no need to speak the rest—
    No need to quiet any fears
Of her—who ask'd no reason why,
But turned on me her quiet eye!

Yet more than worthy of the love
My spirit struggled with, and strove,
When, on the mountain peak, alone,

Ambition lent it a new tone—
I had no being—but in thee:
   The world, and all it did contain
In the earth—the air—the sea—
   Its joy—its little lot of pain
That was new pleasure—the ideal,
   Dim, vanities of dreams by night—
And dimmer nothings which were real—
   (Shadows—and a more shadowy light!)
Parted upon their misty wings,
     And, so, confusedly, became
     Thine image and—a name—a name!
Two separate—yet most intimate things.

I was ambitious—have you known
     The passion, father? You have not:
A cottager, I mark'd a throne
Of half the world as all my own,
     And murmur'd at such lowly lot—
But, just like any other dream,
     Upon the vapor of the dew
My own had past, did not the beam
     Of beauty which did while it thro'
The minute—the hour—the day—oppress
My mind with double loveliness.

We walk'd together on the crown
Of a high mountain which look'd down
Afar from its proud natural towers
   Of rock and forest, on the hills—
The dwindled hills! Begirt with bowers
   And shouting with a thousand rills.

I spoke to her of power and pride,
But mystically—in such guise
That she might deem it nought beside
The moment's converse; in her eyes
I read, perhaps too carelessly,
A mingled feeling with my own—
The flush on her bright cheek, to me
Seem'd to become a queenly throne
Too well that I should let it be
Light in the wilderness alone.
I wrapp'd myself in grandeur then
And donn'd a visionary crown—
Yet it was not that Fantasy
Had thrown her mantle over me—
But that, among the rabble—men,
Lion ambition is chain'd down—
And crouches to a keeper's hand—
Not so in deserts where the grand—
The wild—the terrible conspire
With their own breath to fan his fire.

Look 'round thee now on Samarcand!
Is she not queen of Earth? Her pride
Above all cities? In her hand
Their destinies? In all beside
Of glory which the world hath known
Stands she not nobly and alone?
Falling—her veriest steppingstone
Shall form the pedestal of a throne—
And who her sovereign? Timour—he
Whom the astonished people saw
Striding o'er empires haughtily
A diadem'd outlaw!

O, human love! Thou spirit given,
On Earth, of all we hope in Heaven!
Which fall'st into the soul like rain
Upon the Siroc-wither'd plain,
And, failing in thy power to bless,
But leav'st the heart a wilderness!
Idea! Which bindest life around
With music of so strange a sound
And beauty of so wild a birth—
Farewell! For I have won the Earth.
When Hope, the eagle that tower'd, could see
    No cliff beyond him in the sky,
His pinions were bent droopingly—
    And homeward turn'd his soften'd eye.
'T was sunset: when the sun will part
There comes a sullenness of heart
To him who still would look upon
The glory of the summer sun.
That soul will hate the ev'ning mist
So often lovely, and will list
To the sound of the coming darkness (known
To those whose spirits harken) as one
Who, in a dream of night, *would* fly
But *cannot* from a danger nigh.

What tho' the moon—the white moon—
Shed all the splendor of her noon,
Her smile is chilly—and *her* beam,
In that time of dreariness, will seem
(So like you gather in your breath)
A portrait taken after death.
And boyhood is a summer sun
Whose waning is the dreariest one.

For all we live to know is known,
And all we seek to keep hath flown.
Let life, then, as the day-flower, fall
With the noonday beauty—which is all.

I reach'd my home—my home no more—
    For all had flown who made it so.
I pass'd from out its mossy door,
    And, tho' my tread was soft and low,
A voice came from the threshold stone
Of one whom I had earlier known—
    O, I defy thee, Hell, to show
    On beds of fire that burn below,
    An humbler heart—a deeper wo.

Father, I firmly do believe—
    I *know*—for Death who comes for me
        From regions of the blest afar,
Where there is nothing to deceive,
        Hath left his iron gate ajar,
    And rays of truth you cannot see
    Are flashing thro' Eternity—
I do believe that Eblis hath
A snare in every human path—
Else how, when in the holy grove
I wandered of the idol, Love,
Who daily scents his snowy wings
With incense of burnt offerings

From the most unpolluted things,
Whose pleasant bowers are yet so riven
Above with trellis'd rays from Heaven
No mote may shun—no tiniest fly—

The light'ning of his eagle eye—
How was it that Ambition crept,
    Unseen, amid the revels there,
Till growing bold, he laughed and leapt
    In the tangles of Love's very hair?

SONG

I saw thee on thy bridal day—
    When a burning blush came o'er thee,
Though happiness around thee lay,
    The world all love before thee:

And in thine eye a kindling light
    (Whatever it might be)
Was all on Earth my aching sight
    Of Loveliness could see.

That blush, perhaps, was maiden shame—
    As such it well may pass—
Though its glow hath raised a fiercer flame
    In the breast of him, alas!

Who saw thee on that bridal day,
    When that deep blush *would* come o'er thee,
Though happiness around thee lay,
    The world all love before thee.

DREAMS

Oh! That my young life were a lasting dream!
My spirit not awak'ning till the beam
Of an Eternity should bring the morrow.
Yes! Tho' that long dream were of hopeless sorrow,
'T were better than the cold reality
Of waking life, to him whose heart must be,
And hath been still, upon the lovely earth,
A chaos of deep passion, from his birth.
But should it be—that dream eternally
Continuing—as dreams have been to me
In my young boyhood—should it thus be giv'n,
'T were folly still to hope for higher Heav'n.
For I have revell'd, when the sun was bright
I' the summer sky, in dreams of living light
And loveliness—have left my very heart
In climes of mine imagining, apart
From mine own home, with beings that have been
Of mine own thought—what more could I have seen?
'T was once—and only once—and the wild hour
From my remembrance shall not pass—some pow'r
Or spell had bound me—'t was the chilly wind
Came o'er me in the night, and left behind
Its image on my spirit—or the moon
Shone on my slumbers in her lofty noon
Too coldly—or the stars—howe'er it was,

13

That dream was as that night-wind—let it pass.
I *have been* happy, tho' [but] in a dream.
I have been happy—and I love the theme:
Dreams! In their vivid coloring of life,
As in that fleeting, shadowy, misty strife

Of semblance with reality which brings
To the delirious eye, more lovely things
Of Paradise and Love—and all our own!
Than young Hope in his sunniest hour hath known.

Spirits of the Dead

I

Thy soul shall find itself alone
'Mid dark thoughts of the gray tombstone—
Not one, of all the crowd, to pry
Into thine hour of secrecy.

II

Be silent in that solitude,
    Which is not loneliness—for then
The spirits of the dead who stood
    In life before thee are again
In death around thee—and their will
Shall overshadow thee: be still.

III

The night, tho' clear, shall frown—
And the stars shall look not down
From their high thrones in the heaven,
With light like Hope to mortals given—
But their red orbs, without beam,
To thy weariness shall seem
As a burning and a fever
Which would cling to thee forever.

IV

Now are thoughts thou shalt not banish,
Now are visions ne'er to vanish;
From thy spirit shall they pass
No more—like dewdrop from the grass.

V

The breeze—the breath of God—is still—
And the mist upon the hill,
Shadowy—shadowy—yet unbroken,
Is a symbol and a token—
How it hangs upon the trees,
A mystery of mysteries!

EVENING STAR

'T was noontide of summer,
 And mid-time of night;
And stars, in their orbits,
 Shone pale, thro' the light
Of the brighter, cold moon,
 'Mid planets her slaves,
Herself in the Heavens,
 Her beam on the waves.
 I gaz'd a while
 On her cold smile;
Too cold—too cold for me.
 There pass'd, as a shroud,
 A fleecy cloud,
And I turn'd away to thee,
 Proud Evening Star,
 In thy glory afar,
And dearer thy beam shall be;
 For joy to my heart
 Is the proud part
Thou bearest in Heav'n at night,
 And more I admire
Thy distant fire
Than that colder, lowly light.

A DREAM WITHIN A DREAM

Take this kiss upon the brow!
And, in parting from you now,
Thus much let me avow—
You are not wrong, who deem
That my days have been a dream;
Yet if Hope has flown away
In a night, or in a day,
In a vision, or in none,
Is it therefore the less *gone*?
All that we see or seem
Is but a dream within a dream.

I stand amid the roar
Of a surf-tormented shore,
And I hold within my hand
Grains of the golden sand—
How few! Yet how they creep
Through my fingers to the deep,
While I weep—while I weep!
O God! Can I not grasp
Them with a tighter clasp?
O God! Can I not save
One from the pitiless wave?
Is *all* that we see or seem
But a dream within a dream?

STANZAS

How often we forget all time, when lone
Admiring Nature's universal throne;
Her woods—her wilds—her mountains—the intense
Reply of HERS *to* OUR *intelligence!*

I

In youth have I known one with whom the Earth,
In secret, communing held—as he with it,
In daylight, and in beauty from his birth:
Whose fervid, flick'ring torch of life was lit
From the sun and stars, whence he had drawn forth
A passionate light—such for his spirit was fit—
And yet that spirit knew not—in the hour
Of its own fervor—what had o'er it power.

II

Perhaps it may be that my mind is wrought
To a fever by the moonbeam that hangs o'er,
But I will half believe that wild light fraught
With more of sov'reignty than ancient lore
Hath ever told—or is it of a thought
The unembodied essence, and no more,
That with a quick'ning spell doth o'er us pass
As dew of the nighttime, o'er the summer grass?

III

Doth o'er us pass, when, as th' expanding eye
To the lov'd object—so the tear to the lid
Will start, which lately slept in apathy?
And yet it need not be—(that object) hid
From us in life—but common—which doth lie
Each hour before us—but *then* only, bid
With a strange sound, as of a harp-string broken,
T' awake us—'T is a symbol and a token.

IV

Of what in other worlds shall be—and giv'n
In beauty by our God, to those alone
Who otherwise would fall from life and Heav'n,
Drawn by their heart's passion, and that tone,
That high tone of the spirit which hath striv'n,
Tho' not with Faith—with godliness—whose throne
With desp'rate energy 't hath beaten down;
Wearing its own deep feeling as a crown.

A DREAM

In visions of the dark night
    I have dreamed of joy departed,
But a waking dream of life and light
    Hath left me broken-hearted.

Ah! What is not a dream by day
    To him whose eyes are cast
On things around him with a ray
    Turned back upon the past?

That holy dream—that holy dream,
    While all the world were chiding,
Hath cheered me as a lovely beam
    A lonely spirit guiding.

What though that light, thro' storm and night,
    So trembled from afar,
What could there be more purely bright
    In Truth's daystar?

"The Happiest Day—the Happiest Hour"

The happiest day—the happiest hour
    My sear'd and blighted heart hath known,
The highest hope of pride and power,
    I feel hath flown.

Of power! Said I? Yes! Such I ween;
    But they have vanish'd long, alas!
The visions of my youth have been—
    But let them pass.

And, pride, what have I now with thee?
    Another brow may ev'n inherit
The venom thou hast pour'd on me—
    Be still, my spirit.

The happiest day—the happiest hour
    Mine eyes shall see—have ever seen,
The brightest glance of pride and power
    I feel—have been:

But were that hope of pride and power
    Now offer'd, with the pain
Ev'n *then* I felt—that brightest hour
    I would not live again:

For on its wing was dark alloy,
    And as it flutter'd—fell
An essence—powerful to destroy
    A soul that knew it well.

THE LAKE: TO _____

In spring of youth it was my lot
To haunt of the wide world a spot
The which I could not love the less—
So lovely was the loneliness
Of a wild lake, with black rock bound,
And the tall pines that towered around.

But when the Night had thrown her pall
Upon that spot, as upon all,
And the mystic wind went by
Murmuring in melody,
Then—ah, then—I would awake
To the terror of the lone lake.

Yet that terror was not fright,
But a tremulous delight—
A feeling not the jewelled mine
Could teach or bribe me to define—
Nor Love—although the Love were thine.

Death was in that poisonous wave,
And in its gulf a fitting grave
For him who thence could solace bring
To his lone imagining,
Whose solitary soul could make
An Eden of that dim lake.

Sonnet—To Science

Science! True daughter of Old Time thou art!
    Who alterest all things with thy peering eyes.
Why preyest thou thus upon the poet's heart,
    Vulture, whose wings are dull realities?
How should he love thee? Or how deem thee wise,
    Who wouldst not leave him in his wandering
To seek for treasure in the jewelled skies,
    Albeit he soared with an undaunted wing?
Hast thou not dragged Diana from her car,
    And driven the Hamadryad from the wood,
To seek a shelter in some happier star?
    Hast thou not torn the Naiad from her flood,
The Elfin from the green grass, and from me
The summer dream beneath the tamarind tree?

AL AARAAF

PART I

O! Nothing earthly save the ray
(Thrown back from flowers) of Beauty's eye,
As in those gardens where the day
Springs from the gems of Circassy—
O! Nothing earthly save the thrill
Of melody in woodland rill—
Or (music of the passion-hearted)
Joy's voice so peacefully departed
That, like the murmur in the shell,
Its echo dwelleth and will dwell—
Oh, nothing of the dross of ours—
Yet all the beauty—all the flowers
That list our Love, and deck our bowers—
Adorn yon world afar, afar—
The wandering star.

'T was a sweet time for Nesace—for there
Her world lay lolling on the golden air,
Near four bright suns—a temporary rest—
An oasis in desert of the blest.
Away—away—'mid seas of rays that roll
Empyrean splendor o'er th' unchained soul—
The soul that scarce (the billows are so dense)
Can struggle to its destin'd eminence—

To distant spheres, from time to time, she rode,
And late to ours, the favor'd one of God—
But, now, the ruler of an anchor'd realm,
She throws aside the sceptre—leaves the helm,
And, amid incense and high spiritual hymns,
Laves in quadruple light her angel limbs.

Now happiest, loveliest in yon lovely Earth,
Whence sprang the "Idea of Beauty" into birth
(Falling in wreaths thro' many a startled star,
Like woman's hair 'mid pearls, until, afar,
It lit on hills Achaian, and there dwelt),
She look'd into Infinity—and knelt.
Rich clouds, for canopies, about her curled—
Fit emblems of the model of her world—
Seen but in beauty—not impeding sight
Of other beauty glittering thro' the light—
A wreath that twined each starry form around,
And all the opal'd air in color bound.

All hurriedly she knelt upon a bed
Of flowers: of lilies such as rear'd the head
On the fair Capo Deucato, and sprang
So eagerly around about to hang
Upon the flying footsteps of—deep pride—
Of her who lov'd a mortal—and so died.
The Sephalica, budding with young bees,
Uprear'd its purple stem around her knees:
And gemmy flower, of Trebizond misnam'd—
Inmate of highest stars, where erst it sham'd
All other loveliness: its honied dew
(The fabled nectar that the heathen knew)
Deliriously sweet, was dropp'd from Heaven,

And fell on gardens of the unforgiven
In Trebizond—and on a sunny flower
So like its own above, that, to this hour,
It still remaineth, torturing the bee
With madness, and unwonted reverie:
In Heaven, and all its environs, the leaf
And blossom of the fairy plant, in grief
Disconsolate linger—grief that hangs her head,
Repenting follies that full long have fled,
Heaving her white breast to the balmy air,
Like guilty beauty, chasten'd, and more fair:
Nyctanthes, too, as sacred as the light
She fears to perfume, perfuming the night:
And Clytia pondering between many a sun,
While pettish tears adown her petals run:
And that aspiring flower that sprang on Earth—
And died, ere scarce exalted into birth,
Bursting its odorous heart in spirit to wing
Its way to Heaven, from garden of a king:
And Valisnerian lotus thither flown
From struggling with the waters of the Rhone:
And thy most lovely purple perfume, Zante!
Isola d'oro! Fior di Levante!
And the Nelumbo bud that floats forever
With Indian Cupid down the holy river—
Fair flowers, and fairy! To whose care is given
To bear the Goddess' song, in odours, up to Heaven:

> "Spirit! That dwellest where,
>   In the deep sky,
>   The terrible and fair,
>   In beauty vie!

Beyond the line of blue—
    The boundary of the star
Which turneth at the view
    Of thy barrier and thy bar—
Of the barrier overgone
    By the comets who were cast
From their pride, and from their throne,
    To be drudges till the last—
To be carriers of fire
    (The red fire of their heart)
With speed that may not tire
    And with pain that shall not part—
Who livest—*that* we know—
    In Eternity—we feel—
But the shadow of whose brow
    What spirit shall reveal?
Tho' the beings whom thy Nesace,
    Thy messenger, hath known,
Have dream'd for thy Infinity
    A model of their own—
Thy will is done, Oh, God!
    The star hath ridden high
Thro' many a tempest, but she rode
    Beneath thy burning eye;
And here, in thought, to thee—
    In thought that can alone
Ascend thy empire and so be
    A partner of thy throne—
By winged Fantasy,
    My embassy is given,
Till secrecy shall knowledge be
    In the environs of Heaven."

She ceas'd—and buried then her burning cheek
Abash'd, amid the lilies there, to seek
A shelter from the fervour of His eye;
For the stars trembled at the Deity.
She stirr'd not—breath'd not—for a voice was there
How solemnly pervading the calm air!
A sound of silence on the startled ear
Which dreamy poets name "the music of the sphere."
Ours is a world of words: Quiet we call
"Silence"—which is the merest word of all.
All Nature speaks, and ev'n ideal things
Flap shadowy sounds from visionary wings—
But ah! Not so when, thus, in realms on high
The eternal voice of God is passing by;
And the red winds are withering in the sky!

"What tho' in worlds which sightless cycles run,
Link'd to a little system and one sun—
Where all my love is folly, and the crowd
Still think my terrors but the thunder cloud,
The storm, the earthquake, and the ocean wrath
(Ah! Will they cross me in my angrier path?)—
What tho' in worlds which own a single sun
The sands of Time grow dimmer as they run,
Yet thine is my resplendency, so given
To bear my secrets thro' the upper Heaven.
Leave tenantless thy crystal home, and fly,
With all thy train, athwart the moony sky—
Apart—life fire-flies in Sicilian night,
And wing to other worlds another light!
Divulge the secrets of thy embassy
To the proud orbs that twinkle—and so be

To ev'ry heart a barrier and a ban
Lest the stars totter in the guilt of man!"

Up rose the maiden in the yellow night,
The single-mooned eve! On Earth we plight
Our faith to one love—and one moon adore—
The birthplace of young Beauty had no more.
As sprang that yellow star from downy hours
Up rose the maiden from her shrine of flowers,
And bent o'er sheeny mountain and dim plain
Her way—but left not yet her Therasæan reign.

PART II

High on a mountain of enamell'd head—
Such as the drowsy shepherd on his bed
Of giant pasturage lying at his ease,
Raising his heavy eyelid, starts and sees
With many a mutter'd "hope to be forgiven,"
What time the moon is quadrated in Heaven—
Of rosy head, that towering far away
Into the sunlit ether, caught the ray
Of sunken suns at eve—at noon of night,
While the moon danc'd with the fair stranger light—
Uprear'd upon such height arose a pile
Of gorgeous columns on th' unburthen'd air,
Flashing from Parian marble that twin smile
Far down upon the wave that sparkled there,
And nursled the young mountain in its lair.
Of molten stars their pavement, such as fall
Thro' the ebon air, besilvering the pall
Of their own dissolution, while they die—
Adorning then the dwellings of the sky.

A dome, by linked light from Heaven let down,
Sat gently on these columns as a crown—
A window of one circular diamond, there,
Look'd out above into the purple air,
And rays from God shot down that meteor chain
And hallow'd all the beauty twice again,
Save when, between th' Empyrean and that ring,
Some eager spirit flapp'd his dusky wing.
But on the pillars Seraph eyes have seen
The dimness of this world: that grayish green
That Nature loves the best for Beauty's grave
Lurk'd in each cornice, round each architrave—
And every sculptur'd cherub thereabout
That from his marble dwelling peeréd out,
Seem'd earthly in the shadow of his niche—
Achaian statues in a world so rich!
Friezes from Tadmor and Persepolis,
From Balbec, and the stilly, clear abyss
Of beautiful Gomorrah! O, the wave
Is now upon thee—but too late to save!

Sound loves to revel in a summer night:
Witness the murmur of the gray twilight
That stole upon the ear, in Eyraco,
Of many a wild star gazer long ago—
That stealeth ever on the ear of him
Who, musing, gazeth on the distance dim,
And sees the darkness coming as a cloud—
Is not its form—its voice—most palpable and loud?

But what is this? It cometh—and it brings
A music with it—'t is the rush of wings—
A pause—and then a sweeping, falling strain,
And Nesace in her halls again.

From the wild energy of wanton haste
    Her cheeks were flushing, and her lips apart;
And zone that clung around her gentle waist
    Had burst beneath the heaving of her heart.
Within the centre of that hall to breathe
She paus'd and panted, Zanthe! All beneath,
The fairy light that kiss'd her golden hair
And long'd to rest, yet could but sparkle there!

    Young flowers were whispering in melody
To happy flowers that night—and tree to tree;
Fountains were gushing music as they fell
In many a star-lit grove, or moon-lit dell;
Yet silence came upon material things—
Fair flowers, bright waterfalls, and angel wings—
And sound alone, that from the spirit sprang,
Bore burthen to the charm the maiden sang:

      "'Neath blue-bell or streamer—
        Or tufted wild spray
    That keeps from the dreamer
        The moonbeam away—
    Bright beings! That ponder,
        With half closing eyes,
    On the stars which your wonder
        Hath drawn from the skies,
    Till they glance thro' the shade, and
        Come down to your brow
    Like—eyes of the maiden
        Who calls on you now—
    Arise! From your dreaming
        In violet bowers,
    To duty beseeming
        These star-litten hours—

And shake from your tresses,
  Encumber'd with dew,
The breath of those kisses
  That cumber them too
(O, how, without you, Love!
  Could angels be blest?)—
Those kisses of true love
  That lull'd ye to rest!
Up! Shake from your wing
  Each hindering thing:
The dew of the night—
  It would weigh down your flight;
And true love caresses—
  O! Leave them apart:
They are light on the tresses,
  But lead on the heart.
"Ligeia! Ligeia!
  My beautiful one!
Whose harshest idea
  Will to melody run,
O! Is it thy will
  On the breezes to toss?
Or, capriciously still,
  Like the lone Albatross,
Incumbent on night
  (As she on the air)
To keep watch with delight
  On the harmony there?

"Ligeia! Wherever
  Thy image may be,
No image shall sever
  Thy music from thee.

Thou has bound many eyes
 In a dreamy sleep—
But the strains still arise
 Which *thy* vigilance keep—
The sound of the rain
 Which leaps down to the flower,
And dances again
 In the rhythm of the shower—
The murmur that springs
 From the growing of grass
Are the music of things—
 But are modell'd, alas!
Away, then, my dearest,
 O! Hie thee away
To springs that lie clearest
 Beneath the moon-ray—
To lone lake that smiles,
 In its dream of deep rest,
At the many star-isles
 That enjewel its breast—
Where wild flowers, creeping,
 Have mingled their shade,
On its margin is sleeping
 Full many a maid—
Some have left the cool glade, and
 Have slept with the bee—
Arouse them, my maiden,
 On moorland and lea—
Go! Breathe on their slumber,
 All softly in ear,
The musical number
 They slumber'd to hear—
For what can awaken

An angel so soon,
Whose sleep hath been taken
Beneath the cold moon,
As the spell which no slumber
Of witchery may test,
The rhythmical number
Which lull'd him to rest?"

Spirits in wing, and angels to the view,
A thousand seraphs burst th' Empyrean thro',
Young dreams still hovering on their drowsy flight—
Seraphs in all but "Knowledge," the keen light
That fell, refracted, thro' thy bounds, afar,
O Death! From eye of God upon that star:
Sweet was that error—sweeter still that death—
Sweet was that error—ev'n with *us* the breath
Of Science dims the mirror of our joy—
To them 't were the Simoom, and would destroy—
For what (to them) availeth it to know
That Truth is Falsehood—or that Bliss is Woe?
Sweet was their death—with them to die was rife
With the last ecstasy of satiate life—
Beyond that death no immortality—
But sleep that pondereth and is not "to be"—
And there—oh! May my weary spirit dwell—
Apart from Heaven's Eternity—and yet how far from Hell!

What guilty spirit, in what shrubbery dim,
Heard not the stirring summons of that hymn?
But two: they fell: for Heaven no grace imparts
To those who hear not for their beating hearts.
A maiden-angel and her seraph-lover—
O! Where (and ye may seek the wide skies over)

Was Love, the blind, near sober Duty known?
    Unguided Love hath fallen—'mid "tears of perfect moan."

    He was a goodly spirit—he who fell:
A wanderer by moss-y-mantled well—
A gazer on the lights that shine above—
A dreamer in the moonbeam by his love:
What wonder? For each star is eye-like there,
And looks so sweetly down on Beauty's hair;
And they, and ev'ry mossy spring were holy
To his love-haunted heart and melancholy.
The night had found (to him a night of wo)
Upon a mountain crag, young Angelo—
Beetling it bends athwart the solemn sky,
And scowls on starry worlds that down beneath it lie.
Here sate he with his love—his dark eye bent
With eagle gaze along the firmament:
Now turn'd it upon her—but ever then
It trembled to the orb of EARTH again.

    "Ianthe, dearest, see! How dim that ray!
How lovely 't is to look so far away!
She seemed not thus upon that autumn eve
I left her gorgeous halls—nor mourn'd to leave.
That eve—that eve—I should remember well—
The sun-ray dropp'd, in Lemnos, with a spell
On th' Arabesque carving of a gilded hall
Wherein I sate, and on the draperied wall—
And on my eyelids—O the heavy light!
How drowsily it weigh'd them into night!
On flowers, before, and mist, and love they ran
With Persian Saadi in his Gulistan:
But O that light! I slumber'd—Death, the while,

Stole o'er my senses in that lovely isle
So softly that no single silken hair
Awoke that slept—or knew that he was there.

    "The last spot of Earth's orb I trod upon
Was a proud temple call'd the Parthenon.
More beauty clung around her column'd wall
Than ev'n thy glowing bosom beats withal,
And when old Time my wing did disenthral—
Thence sprang I—as the eagle from his tower,
And years I left behind me in an hour.
What time upon her airy bounds I hung,
One half the garden of her globe was flung,
Unrolling as a chart unto my view—
Tenantless cities of the desert too!
Ianthe, beauty crowded on me then,
And half I wish'd to be again of men."

    "My Angelo! And why of them to be?
A brighter dwelling-place is here for thee—
And greener fields than in yon world above,
And woman's loveliness—and passionate love."

    "But, list, Ianthe! When the air so soft
Fail'd, as my pennon'd spirit leapt aloft,
Perhaps my brain grew dizzy—but the world
I left so late was into chaos hurl'd—
Sprang from her station, on the winds apart,
And roll'd, a flame, the fiery Heaven athwart.
Methought, my sweet one, then I ceased to soar,
And fell—not swiftly as I rose before,
But with a downward, tremulous motion thro'
Light, brazen rays, this golden star unto!

Nor long the measure of my falling hours,
For nearest of all stars was thine to ours—
Dread star! That came, amid a night of mirth,
A red Dædalion on the timid Earth."

   "We came—and to thy Earth—but not to us
Be given our lady's bidding to discuss:
We came, my love; around, above, below,
Gay fire-fly of the night we come and go,
Nor ask a reason save the angel-nod
She grants to us, as granted by her God—
   But, Angelo, than thine gray Time unfurl'd
Never his fairy wing o'er fairier world!
Dim was its little disk, and angel eyes
Alone could see the phantom in the skies,
When first Al Aaraaf knew her course to be
Headlong thitherward o'er the starry sea—
But when its glory swell'd upon the sky,
As glowing Beauty's bust beneath man's eye,
We paus'd before the heritage of men,
And thy star trembled—as doth Beauty then!"

   Thus, in discourse, the lovers whiled away
The night that waned and waned and brought no day.
They fell: for Heaven to them no hope imparts
Who hear not for the beating of their hearts.

ROMANCE

Romance, who loves to nod and sing,
With drowsy head and folded wing,
Among the green leaves as they shake
Far down within some shadowy lake,
To me a painted paroquet
Hath been—a most familiar bird—
Taught me my alphabet to say—
To lisp my very earliest word
While in the wild wood I did lie,
A child—with a most knowing eye.
Of late, eternal Condor years
So shake the very Heaven on high
With tumult as they thunder by,
I have no time for idle cares
Through gazing on the unquiet sky.
And when an hour with calmer wings
Its down upon my spirit flings—
That little time with lyre and rhyme
To while away—forbidden things!
My heart would feel to be a crime
Unless it trembled with the strings.

To ⸺

The bowers whereat, in dreams, I see
   The wantonest singing birds,
Are lips—and all thy melody
   Of lip-begotten words.

Thine eyes, in Heaven of heart enshrined,
   Then desolately fall,
O God! On my funereal mind
   Like starlight on a pall.

Thy heart—*thy* heart! I wake and sigh,
   And sleep to dream till day
Of the truth that gold can never buy—
   Of the baubles that it may.

TO THE RIVER

Fair river! In thy bright, clear flow
    Of crystal, wandering water,
Thou art an emblem of the glow
       Of beauty—the unhidden heart—
       The playful maziness of art
    In old Alberto's daughter;
But when within thy wave she looks—
    Which glistens then, and trembles—
Why, then, the prettiest of brooks
    Her worshipper resembles;
For in his heart, as in thy stream,
    Her image deeply lies—
His heart which trembles at the beam
    Of her soul-searching eyes.

To ⸻

I heed not that my earthly lot
    Hath—little of Earth in it—
That years of love have been forgot
    In the hatred of a minute:
I mourn not that the desolate
    Are happier, sweet, than I,
But that *you* sorrow for my fate
    Who am a passer by.

FAIRY-LAND

Dim vales—and shadowy floods—
And cloudy-looking woods,
Whose forms we can't discover
For the tears that drip all over:
Huge moons there wax and wane—
Again—again—again—
Every moment of the night—
Forever changing places—
And they put out the star-light
With the breath from their pale faces.
About twelve by the moon-dial,
One more filmy than the rest
(A kind which, upon trial,
They have found to be the best)
Comes down—still down—and down
With its centre on the crown
Of a mountain's eminence,
While its wide circumference
In easy drapery falls
Over hamlets, over halls,
Wherever they may be—
O'er the strange woods—o'er the sea—
Over spirits on the wing—
Over every drowsy thing—
And buries them up quite

In a labyrinth of light—
And then, how deep! O, deep,
Is the passion of their sleep.
In the morning they arise,
And their moony covering
Is soaring in the skies,
With the tempests as they toss,
Like—almost any thing—
Or a yellow Albatross.
They use that moon no more
For the same end as before,
Videlicet, a tent—
Which I think extravagant:
Its atomies, however,
Into a shower dissever,
Of which those butterflies
Of Earth, who seek the skies,
And so come down again
(Never-contented things!)
Have brought a specimen
Upon their quivering wings.

To Helen

Helen, thy beauty is to me
    Like those Nicéan barks of yore,
That gently, o'er a perfumed sea,
    The weary, way-worn wanderer bore
    To his own native shore.

On desperate seas long wont to roam,
    Thy hyacinth hair, thy classic face,
Thy Naiad airs have brought me home
    To the glory that was Greece,
    And the grandeur that was Rome.

Lo! In yon brilliant window-niche
    How statue-like I see thee stand,
    The agate lamp within thy hand!
Ah, Psyche, from the regions which
    Are Holy Land!

ISRAFEL

And the angel Israfel, whose heartstrings are a lute, and who has the sweetest voice of all God's creatures.

—KORAN

In Heaven a spirit doth dwell
    "Whose heartstrings are a lute";
None sings so wildly well
As the angel Israfel,
And the giddy stars (so legends tell),
Ceasing their hymns, attend the spell
    Of his voice, all mute.

Tottering above
    In her highest noon,
    The enamoured moon
Blushes with love,
    While, to listen, the red levin
    (With the rapid Pleiads, even,
    Which were seven,)
    Pauses in Heaven.

And they say (the starry choir
    And the other listening things)
That Israfeli's fire
Is owing to that lyre

By which he sits and sings—
The trembling living wire
    Of those unusual strings.

But the skies that angel trod,
    Where deep thoughts are a duty,
Where Love's a grown-up God,
    Where the Houri glances are
Imbued with all the beauty
    Which we worship in a star.

Therefore, thou art not wrong,
    Israfeli, who despisest
An unimpassioned song;
To thee the laurels belong,
    Best bard, because the wisest!
Merrily live, and long!

The ecstasies above
    With thy burning measures suit—
Thy grief, thy joy, thy hate, thy love,
    With the fervour of thy lute—
    Well may the stars be mute!

Yes, Heaven is thine; but this
    Is a world of sweets and sours;
    Our flowers are merely—flowers,
And the shadow of thy perfect bliss
    Is the sunshine of ours.

If I could dwell
Where Israfel
    Hath dwelt, and he where I,

He might not sing so wildly well
    A mortal melody,
While a bolder note than this might swell
    From my lyre within the sky.

THE CITY IN THE SEA

Lo! Death has reared himself a throne
In a strange city lying alone
Far down within the dim West,
Where the good and the bad and the worst and the best
Have gone to their eternal rest.
There shrines and palaces and towers
(Time-eaten towers that tremble not!)
Resemble nothing that is ours.
Around, by lifting winds forgot,
Resignedly beneath the sky
The melancholy waters lie.

No rays from the holy heaven come down
On the long nighttime of that town;
But light from out the lurid sea
Streams up the turrets silently—
Gleams up the pinnacles far and free—
Up domes—up spires—up kingly halls—
Up fanes—up Babylon-like walls—
Up shadowy long-forgotten bowers
Of sculptured ivy and stone flowers—
Up many and many a marvellous shrine
Whose wreathéd friezes intertwine
The viol, the violet, and the vine.

Resignedly beneath the sky
The melancholy waters lie.
So blend the turrets and shadows there
That all seem pendulous in air,
While from a proud tower in the town
Death looks gigantically down.

There open fanes and gaping graves
Yawn level with the luminous waves;
But not the riches there that lie
In each idol's diamond eye—
Not the gaily-jewelled dead
Tempt the waters from their bed;
For no ripples curl, alas!
Along that wilderness of glass—
No swellings tell that winds may be
Upon some far-off happier sea—
No heavings hint that winds have been
On seas less hideously serene.

But lo, a stir is in the air!
The wave—there is a movement there!
As if the towers had thrust aside,
In slightly sinking, the dull tide—
As if their tops had feebly given
A void within the filmy Heaven.
The waves have now a redder glow—
The hours are breathing faint and low—
And when, amid no earthly moans,
Down, down that town shall settle hence,
Hell, rising from a thousand thrones,
Shall do it reverence.

THE SLEEPER

At midnight, in the month of June,
I stand beneath the mystic moon.
An opiate vapor, dewy, dim,
Exhales from out her golden rim,
And softly dripping, drop by drop,
Upon the quiet mountain top,
Steals drowsily and musically
Into the universal valley.
The rosemary nods upon the grave;
The lily lolls upon the wave;
Wrapping the fog about its breast,
The ruin moulders into rest;
Looking like Lethe, see! The lake
A conscious slumber seems to take,
And would not, for the world, awake.
All Beauty sleeps! And lo! Where lies
Irene, with her Destinies!

Oh, lady bright! Can it be right—
This window open to the night?
The wanton airs, from the treetop,
Laughingly through the lattice drop—
The bodiless airs, a wizard rout,
Flit through thy chamber in and out,
And wave the curtain canopy

So fitfully—so fearfully—
Above the closed and fringed lid
'Neath which thy slumb'ring soul lies hid,
That, o'er the floor and down the wall,
Like ghosts the shadows rise and fall!
Oh, lady dear, hast thou no fear?
Why and what art thou dreaming here?
Sure thou art come o'er far-off seas,
A wonder to these garden trees!
Strange is thy pallor! Strange thy dress!
Strange, above all, thy length of tress,
And this all solemn silentness!

The lady sleeps! Oh, may her sleep,
Which is enduring, so be deep!
Heaven have her in its sacred keep!
This chamber changed for one more holy,
This bed for one more melancholy,
I pray to God that she may lie
Forever with unopened eye,
While the pale sheeted ghosts go by!

My love, she sleeps! Oh, may her sleep,
As it is lasting, so be deep!
Soft may the worms about her creep!
Far in the forest, dim and old,
For her may some tall vault unfold—
Some vault that oft hath flung its black
And wingéd pannels fluttering back,
Triumphant, o'er the crested palls
Of her grand family funerals—

Some sepulchre, remote, alone,
Against whose portals she hath thrown,

In childhood, many an idle stone—
Some tomb from out whose sounding door
She ne'er shall force an echo more,
Thrilling to think, poor child of sin!
It was the dead who groaned within.

LENORE

Ah, broken is the golden bowl! The spirit flown forever!
Let the bell toll! A saintly soul floats on the Stygian river;
And, Guy De Vere, hast *thou* no tear? Weep now or never more!
See! On yon drear and rigid bier low lies thy love, Lenore!
Come, let the burial rite be read—the funeral song be sung!
An anthem for the queenliest dead that ever died so young—
A dirge for her the doubly dead in that she died so young.

"Wretches! Ye loved her for her wealth and ye hated her for
      her pride,
And, when she fell in feeble health, ye blessed her—that she died:
How shall the ritual, then, be read? The requiem how be sung
By you—by yours, the evil eye, by yours, the slanderous tongue
That did to death the innocence that died, and died so young?"

Peccavimus; yet rave not thus! But let a Sabbath song
Go up to God so solemnly the dead may feel no wrong!
The sweet Lenore "hath gone before," with Hope that flew beside,
Leaving thee wild for the dear child that should have been
      thy bride—
For her, the fair and *debonair,* that now so lowly lies,
The life upon her yellow hair, but not within her eyes—
The life still there upon her hair—the death upon her eyes.

"Avaunt! Avaunt! From fiends below the indignant ghost is riven—
From Hell unto a high estate far up within the Heaven—

From grief and groan to a golden throne beside the King
    of Heaven!
Let *no* bell toll, then! Lest her soul, amid its hallowed mirth,
Should catch the note as it doth float up from the damnéd Earth!
And I! Tonight my heart is light! No dirge will I upraise,
But waft the angel on her flight with a Paean of old days!"

THE VALLEY OF UNREST

Once it smiled a silent dell
Where the people did not dwell;
They had gone unto the wars,
Trusting to the mild-eyed stars,
Nightly, from their azure towers,
To keep watch above the flowers,
In the midst of which all day
The red sun-light lazily lay.
Now each visitor shall confess
The sad valley's restlessness.
Nothing there is motionless—
Nothing save the airs that brood
Over the magic solitude.
Ah, by no wind are stirred those trees
That palpitate like the chill seas
Around the misty Hebrides!
Ah, by no wind those clouds are driven
That rustle through the unquiet Heaven
Uneasily, from morn till even,
Over the violets that lie
In myriad types of the human eye—
Over the lilies there that wave
And weep above a nameless grave!
They wave: from out their fragrant tops

External dews come down in drops.
They weep: from off their delicate stems
Perennial tears descend in gems.

The Coliseum

Type of the antique Rome! Rich reliquary
Of lofty contemplation left to Time
By buried centuries of pomp and power!
At length—at length—after so many days
Of weary pilgrimage and burning thirst
(Thirst for the springs of lore that in thee lie),
I kneel, an altered and an humble man,
Amid thy shadows, and so drink within
My very soul thy grandeur, gloom, and glory!

Vastness! And Age! And Memories of Eld!
Silence! And Desolation! And dim Night!
I feel ye now—I feel ye in your strength—
O spells more sure than e'er Judæan king
Taught in the garden of Gethsemane!
O charms more potent than the rapt Chaldee
Ever drew down from out the quiet stars!

Here, where a hero fell, a column falls!
Here, where the mimic eagle glared in gold,
A midnight vigil holds the swarthy bat!
Here, where the dames of Rome their gilded hair
Waved to the wind, now wave the reed and thistle!
Here, where on golden throne the monarch lolled,
Glides, spectre-like, unto his marble home,

Lit by the wan light of the horned moon,
The swift and silent lizard of the stones!
But stay! These walls—these ivy-clad arcades—
These mouldering plinths—these sad and blackened shafts—
These vague entablatures—this crumbling frieze—
These shattered cornices—this wreck—this ruin—
These stones—alas! These gray stones—are they all—
All of the famed and the colossal left
By the corrosive Hours to Fate and me?

"Not all"—the Echoes answer me—"not all!
Prophetic sounds and loud, arise forever
From us, and from all Ruin, unto the wise,
As melody from Memnon to the Sun.
We rule the hearts of mightiest men—we rule
With a despotic sway all giant minds.
We are not impotent—we pallid stones.
Not all our power is gone—not all our fame—
Not all the magic of our high renown—
Not all the wonder that encircles us—
Not all the mysteries that in us lie—
Not all the memories that hang upon
And cling around about us as a garment,
Clothing us in a robe of more than glory."

To One in Paradise

Thou wast that all to me, love,
    For which my soul did pine—
A green isle in the sea, love,
    A fountain and a shrine,
All wreathed with fairy fruits and flowers,
    And all the flowers were mine.

Ah, dream too bright to last!
    Ah, starry Hope! That didst arise
But to be overcast!
    A voice from out the Future cries,
"On! On!" but o'er the Past
    (Dim gulf!) my spirit hovering lies
Mute, motionless, aghast!

For, alas! Alas! With me
    The light of Life is o'er!
No more—no more—no more—
    (Such language holds the solemn sea
To the sands upon the shore)
    Shall bloom the thunder-blasted tree,
Or the stricken eagle soar!

And all my days are trances,
    And all my nightly dreams

Are where thy gray eye glances,
    And where thy footstep gleams—
In what ethereal dances,
    By what eternal streams.

Hymn

At morn—at noon—at twilight dim—
Maria! Thou hast heard my hymn!
In joy and wo—in good and ill—
Mother of God, be with me still!
When the Hours flew brightly by,
And not a cloud obscured the sky,
My soul, lest it should truant be,
Thy grace did guide to thine and thee;
Now, when storms of Fate o'ercast
Darkly my Present and my Past,
Let my Future radiant shine
With sweet hopes of thee and thine!

To F 

Beloved! Amid the earnest woes
    That crowd around my earthly path—
(Drear path, alas! Where grows
Not even one lonely rose)—
    My soul at least a solace hath
In dreams of thee, and therein knows
An Eden of bland repose.

And thus thy memory is to me
    Like some enchanted far-off isle
In some tumultuous sea—
Some ocean throbbing far and free
    With storms—but where meanwhile
Serenest skies continually
Just o'er that one bright island smile.

To F ———s S. O ———d

Thou wouldst be loved? Then let thy heart
    From its present pathway part not!
Being everything which now thou art,
    Be nothing which thou art not.
So with the world thy gentle ways,
    Thy grace, thy more than beauty,
Shall be an endless theme of praise,
    And love—a simple duty.

BRIDAL BALLAD

The ring is on my hand,
     And the wreath is on my brow;
Satins and jewels grand
Are all at my command,
     And I am happy now.

And my lord he loves me well;
     But, when first he breathed his vow,
I felt my bosom swell—
For the words rang as a knell,
And the voice seemed *his* who fell
In the battle down the dell,
     And who is happy now.

But he spoke to re-assure me,
     And he kissed my pallid brow,
While a reverie came o'er me,
And to the churchyard bore me,
And I sighed to him before me
(Thinking him dead D'Elormie),
     "Oh, I am happy now!"

And thus the words were spoken,
     And this the plighted vow;
And, though my faith be broken,

And, though my heart be broken,
Here is a ring, as token
    That I am happy now!
Behold the golden token
    That *proves* me happy now!
Would God I could awaken!
    For I dream I know not how,
And my soul is sorely shaken
Lest an evil step be taken,
Lest the dead who is forsaken
    May not be happy now.

SONNET—TO ZANTE

Fair isle, that from the fairest of all flowers
    Thy gentlest of all gentle names dost take,
How many memories of what radiant hours
    At sight of thee and thine at once awake!
How many scenes of what departed bliss!
    How many thoughts of what entombéd hopes!
How many visions of a maiden that is
    No more—no more upon thy verdant slopes!
No more! Alas, that magical sad sound
    Transforming all! Thy charms shall please no *more,*
Thy memory *no more!* Acccurséd ground
    Henceforth I hold thy flower-enamelled shore,
O hyacinthine isle! O purple Zante!
"Isola d'oro! Fior di Levante!"

THE HAUNTED PALACE

In the greenest of our valleys
    By good angels tenanted,
Once a fair and stately palace—
    Radiant palace—reared its head.
In the monarch Thought's dominion,
    It stood there!
Never seraph spread a pinion
    Over fabric half so fair!

Banners yellow, glorious, golden,
    On its roof did float and flow
(This—all this—was in the olden
    Time long ago),
And every gentle air that dallied,
    In that sweet day,
Along the ramparts plumed and pallid,
    A wingéd odor went away.

Wanderers in that happy valley,
    Through two luminous windows, saw
Spirits moving musically,
    To a lute's well-tunéd law,
Round about a throne where, sitting,
    Porphyrogene,
In state his glory well befitting,
    The ruler of the realm was seen.

And all with pearl and ruby glowing
    Was the fair palace door,
Through which came flowing, flowing, flowing,
    And sparkling evermore,
A troop of Echoes, whose sweet duty
    Was but to sing,
In voices of surpassing beauty,
    The wit and wisdom of their king.

But evil things, in robes of sorrow,
    Assailed the monarch's high estate.
(Ah, let us mourn! For never morrow
    Shall dawn upon him, desolate!)
And round about his home the glory
    That blushed and bloomed,
Is but a dim-remembered story
    Of the old time entombed.

And travellers, now, within that valley,
    Through the red-litten windows see
Vast forms that move fantastically
    To a discordant melody,
While, like a ghastly rapid river,
    Through the pale door
A hideous throng rush out forever,
    And laugh—but smile no more.

Sonnet—Silence

There are some qualities—some incorporate things,
  That have a double life, which thus is made
A type of that twin entity which springs
  From matter and light, evinced in solid and shade.
There is a two-fold *Silence*—sea and shore—
  Body and soul. One dwells in lonely places,
  Newly with grass o'ergrown; some solemn graces,
Some human memories and tearful lore,
Render him terrorless: his name's "No More."
He is the corporate Silence: dread him not!
  No power hath he of evil in himself;
But should some urgent fate (untimely lot!)
  Bring thee to meet his shadow (nameless elf,
That haunteth the lone regions where hath trod
No foot of man), commend thyself to God!

THE CONQUEROR WORM

Lo! 'T is a gala night
    Within the lonesome latter years!
An angel throng, bewinged, bedight
    In veils, and drowned in tears,
Sit in a theatre, to see
    A play of hopes and fears,
While the orchestra breathes fitfully
    The music of the spheres.

Mimes, in the form of God on high,
    Mutter and mumble low,
And hither and thither fly—
    Mere puppets they, who come and go
At bidding of vast formless things
    That shift the scenery to and fro,
Flapping from out their Condor wings
    Invisible Wo!

That motley drama—oh, be sure
    It shall not be forgot!
With its Phantom chased for evermore
    By a crowd that seize it not,
Through a circle that ever returneth in
    To the self-same spot,
And much of Madness, and more of Sin,
    And Horror the soul of the plot.

But see, amid the mimic rout,
    A crawling shape intrude!
A blood-red thing that writhes from out
    The scenic solitude!
It writhes! It writhes! With mortal pangs
The mimes become its food,
And seraphs sob at vermin fangs
    In human gore imbued.

Out—out are the lights—out all!
    And, over each quivering form,
The curtain, a funeral pall,
    Comes down with the rush of a storm,
While the angels, all pallid and wan,
    Uprising, unveiling, affirm
That the play is the tragedy, "Man,"
    And its hero, the Conqueror Worm.

DREAM-LAND

By a route obscure and lonely,
Haunted by ill angels only,
Where an Eidolon, named NIGHT,
On a black throne reigns upright,
I have reached these lands but newly
From an ultimate dim Thule—
From a wild weird clime that lieth, sublime,
       Out of SPACE—out of TIME.

Bottomless vales and boundless floods,
And chasms, and caves, and Titan woods,
With forms that no man can discover
For the tears that drip all over;
Mountains toppling evermore
Into seas without a shore;
Seas that restlessly aspire,
Surging, unto skies of fire;
Lakes that endlessly outspread
Their lone waters—lone and dead,
Their still waters—still and chilly
With the snows of the lolling lily.

By the lakes that thus outspread
Their lone waters, lone and dead,
Their sad waters, sad and chilly
With the snows of the lolling lily,

By the mountains—near the river
Murmuring lowly, murmuring ever,
By the grey woods, by the swamp
Where the toad and the newt encamp,
By the dismal tarns and pools
    Where dwell the Ghouls,
By each spot the most unholy—
In each nook most melancholy,
There the traveller meets, aghast,
Sheeted Memories of the Past—
Shrouded forms that start and sigh
As they pass the wanderer by—
White-robed forms of friends long given,
In agony, to the Earth—and Heaven.

For the heart whose woes are legion
'T is a peaceful, soothing region—
For the spirit that walks in shadow
'T is—oh, 't is an Eldorado!
But the traveller, travelling through it,
May not—dare not openly view it;
Never its mysteries are exposed
To the weak human eye unclosed;
So wills its King, who hath forbid
The uplifting of the fringéd lid;
And thus the sad Soul that here passes
Beholds it but through darkened glasses.

By a route obscure and lonely,
Haunted by ill angels only,
Where an Eidolon, named NIGHT,
On a black throne reigns upright,
I have wandered home but newly
From this ultimate dim Thule.

THE RAVEN

Once upon a midnight dreary, while I pondered, weak and weary,
Over many a quaint and curious volume of forgotten lore—
While I nodded, nearly napping, suddenly there came a tapping,
As of some one gently rapping, rapping at my chamber door.
"'T is some visitor," I muttered, "tapping at my chamber door—
        Only this and nothing more."

Ah, distinctly I remember it was in the bleak December;
And each separate dying ember wrought its ghost upon the floor.
Eagerly I wished the morrow; vainly I had sought to borrow
From my books surcease of sorrow—sorrow for the lost Lenore—
For the rare and radiant maiden whom the angels name Lenore—
        Nameless *here* for evermore.

And the silken, sad, uncertain rustling of each purple curtain
Thrilled me—filled me with fantastic terrors never felt before;
So that now, to still the beating of my heart, I stood repeating,
"'T is some visitor entreating entrance at my chamber door—
Some late visitor entreating entrance at my chamber door;
        This it is and nothing more."

Presently my soul grew stronger; hesitating then no longer,
"Sir," said I, "or Madam, truly your forgiveness I implore;
But the fact is I was napping, and so gently you came rapping,
And so faintly you came tapping, tapping at my chamber door,

That I scarce was sure I heard you"—here I opened the door;
        Darkness there and nothing more.

Deep into that darkness peering, long I stood there wonder-
    ing, fearing,
Doubting, dreaming dreams no mortal ever dared to dream before;
But the silence was unbroken, and the stillness gave no token,
And the only word there spoken was the whispered word, "Lenore?"
This I whispered, and an echo murmured back the word "Lenore!"
        Merely this and nothing more.

Back into the chamber turning, all my soul within me burning,
Soon again I heard a tapping somewhat louder than before.
"Surely," said I, "surely that is something at my window lattice;
Let me see, then, what thereat is, and this mystery explore—
Let my heart be still a moment and this mystery explore;
        'T is the wind and nothing more!"

Open here I flung the shutter, when, with many a flirt and flutter,
In there stepped a stately Raven of the saintly days of yore;
Not the least obeisance made he; not a minute stopped or
    stayed he;
But, with mien of lord or lady, perched above my chamber door—
Perched upon a bust of Pallas just above my chamber door—
        Perched, and sat, and nothing more.

Then this ebony bird beguiling my sad fancy into smiling,
By the grave and stern decorum of the countenance it wore,
"Though thy crest be shorn and shaven, thou," I said, "art sure
    no craven,
Ghastly grim and ancient Raven wandering from the Nightly
    shore—
Tell me what thy lordly name is on the Night's Plutonian shore!"
        Quoth the Raven, "Nevermore."

Much I marvelled this ungainly fowl to hear discourse so plainly,
Though its answer little meaning—little relevancy bore;
For we cannot help agreeing that no living human being
Ever yet was blessed with seeing bird above his chamber door—
Bird or beast upon the sculptured bust above his chamber door,
With such name as "Nevermore."

But the Raven, sitting lonely on the placid bust, spoke only
That one word, as if his soul in that one word he did outpour.
Nothing farther then the uttered—not a feather then he
fluttered—
Till I scarcely more than muttered, "Other friends have flown
before—
On the morrow he will leave me, as my Hopes have flown before."
Then the bird said, "Nevermore."

Startled at the stillness broken by reply so aptly spoken,
"Doubtless," said I, "what it utters is its only stock and store
Caught from some unhappy master whom unmerciful Disaster
Followed fast and followed faster till his songs one burden
bore—
Till the dirges of his Hope that melancholy burden bore
Of 'Never—nevermore.'"

But the Raven still beguiling my sad fancy into smiling,
Straight I wheeled a cushioned seat in front of bird and bust
and door;
Then, upon the velvet sinking, I betook myself to linking
Fancy unto fancy, thinking what this ominous bird of yore—
What this grim, ungainly, ghastly, gaunt, and ominous bird of yore
Meant in croaking "Nevermore."

This I sat engaged in guessing, but no syllable expressing
To the fowl whose fiery eyes now burned into my bosom's core;

This and more I sat divining, with my head at ease reclining
On the cushion's velvet lining that the lamp-light gloated o'er,
But whose velvet-violet lining with the lamp-light gloating o'er,
       She shall press, ah, nevermore!

Then, methought, the air grew denser, perfumed from an
    unseen censer
Swung by seraphim whose foot-falls tinkled on the tufted floor.
"Wretch," I cried, "thy God hath lent thee—by these angels he
    hath sent thee
Respite—respite and nepenthe from thy memories of Lenore;
Quaff, oh, quaff this kind nepenthe and forget this lost Lenore!"
       Quoth the Raven, "Nevermore."

"Prophet!" said I. "Thing of evil! Prophet still, if bird or devil!
Whether Tempter sent, or whether tempest tossed thee
    here ashore,
Desolate yet all undaunted, on this desert land enchanted—
On this home by Horror haunted—tell me truly, I implore—
Is there—*is* there balm in Gilead? Tell me—tell me, I implore!"
       Quoth the Raven, "Nevermore."

"Prophet!" said I. "Thing of evil! Prophet still, if bird or devil!
By that Heaven that bends above us—by that God we both adore—
Tell this soul with sorrow laden if, within the distant Aidenn,
It shall clasp a sainted maiden whom the angels name Lenore—
Clasp a rare and radiant maiden whom the angels name Lenore."
       Quoth the Raven, "Nevermore."

"Be that word our sign of parting, bird or fiend!" I shrieked,
    upstarting—
"Get thee back into the tempest and the Night's Plutonian shore!
Leave no black plume as a token of that lie thy soul hath spoken!

Leave my loneliness unbroken! Quit the bust above my door!
Take thy beak from out my heart, and take thy form from off
    my door!"
                    Quoth the Raven, "Nevermore."

And the Raven, never flitting, still is sitting, *still* is sitting
On the pallid bust of Pallas just above my chamber door;
And his eyes have all the seeming of a demon's that is dreaming,
And the lamp-light o'er him streaming throws his shadow on
    the floor;
And my soul from out that shadow that lies floating on the floor
                    Shall be lifted—nevermore!

EULALIE—A SONG

I dwelt alone
In a world of moan,
And my soul was a stagnant tide,
Till the fair and gentle Eulalie became my blushing bride—
Till the yellow-haired young Eulalie became my smiling bride.

Ah, less—less bright
The stars of the night
Than the eyes of the radiant girl!
And never a flake
That the vapor can make
With the moon-tints of purple and pearl,
Can vie with the modest Eulalie's most unregarded curl—
Can compare with the bright-eyed Eulalie's most humble and
careless curl.

Now Doubt—now Pain
Come never again,
For her soul gives me sigh for sigh,
And all day long
Shines, bright and strong,
Astarte within the sky,
While ever to her dear Eulalie upturns her matron eye—
While ever to her young Eulalie upturns her violet eye.

A Valentine

For her these lines are penned, whose luminous eyes,
　　Brightly expressive as the twins of Lœda,
Shall find her own sweet name that, nestling, lies
　　Upon this page, enwrapped from every reader.
Search narrowly this rhyme, which holds a treasure
　　Divine—a talisman—an amulet
That must be worn at heart. Search well the measure;
　　The words—the letters themselves. Do not forget
The trivialest point, or you may lose your labor.
　　And yet there is in this no Gordian knot
Which one might not undo without a sabre,
　　If one could merely understand the plot.
Enwritten upon this page whereon are peering
　　Such eager eyes, there lies, I say, *perdu,*
A well-known name, oft uttered in the hearing
　　Of poets, by poets; as the name is a poet's, too.
Its letters, although naturally lying—
　　Like the knight Pinto (Mendez Ferdinando)—
Still form a synonym for truth. Cease trying!
　　You will not read the riddle though you do the best you *can* do.

To M. L. S _____

Of all who hail thy presence as the morning—
Of all to whom thine absence is the night—
The blotting utterly from out high heaven
The sacred sun—of all who, weeping, bless thee
Hourly for hope—for life—ah! Above all,
For the resurrection of deep-buried faith
In Truth, in Virtue, in Humanity—
Of all who, on Despair's unhallowed bed
Lying down to die, have suddenly arisen
At thy soft-murmured words, "Let there be light!"
At the soft-murmured words that were fulfilled
In the seraphic glancing of thine eyes—
Of all who owe thee most—whose gratitude
Nearest resembles worship—oh, remember
The truest—the most fervently devoted,
And think that these weak lines are written by him—
By him who, as he pens them, thrills to think
His spirit is communing with an angel's.

ULALUME—A BALLAD

The skies they were ashen and sober;
    The leaves they were crispéd and sere—
    The leaves they were withering and sere:
It was night, in the lonesome October
    Of my most immemorial year:
It was hard by the dim lake of Auber,
    In the misty mid region of Weir—
It was down by the dank tarn of Auber,
    In the ghoul-haunted woodland of Weir.

Here once, through an alley Titanic,
    Of cypress, I roamed with my Soul—
    Of cypress, with Psyche, my Soul.
These were days when my heart was volcanic
    As the scoriac rivers that roll—
    As the lavas that restlessly roll—
Their sulphurous currents down Yaanek
    In the ultimate climes of the Pole—
That groan as they roll down Mount Yaanek
    In the realms of the Boreal Pole.

Our talk had been serious and sober,
    But our thoughts they were palsied and sere—
    Our memories were treacherous and sere;
For we knew not the month was October,

And we marked not the night of the year
    (Ah, night of all nights in the year!)—
We noted not the dim lake of Auber
    (Though once we had journeyed down here)—
We remembered not the dank tarn of Auber,
    Nor the ghoul-haunted woodland of Weir.

And now, as the night was senescent
    And star-dials pointed to morn—
    As the star-dials hinted of morn—
At the end of our path a liquescent
    And nebulous lustre was born,
Out of which a miraculous crescent
    Arose with a duplicate horn—
Astarte's bediamonded crescent
    Distinct with its duplicate horn.

And I said: "She is warmer than Dian;
    She rolls through an ether of sighs—
    She revels in a region of sighs.
She has seen that the tears are not dry on
    These cheeks, where the worm never dies,
And has come past the stars of the Lion,
    To point us the path to the skies—
    To the Lethean peace of the skies—
Come up, in despite of the Lion,
    To shine on us with her bright eyes—
Come up through the lair of the Lion,
    With love in her luminous eyes."

But Psyche, uplifting her finger,
    Said: "Sadly this star I mistrust—
    Her pallor I strangely mistrust:

Ah, hasten! Ah, let us not linger!
    Ah, fly! Let us fly! For we must."
In terror she spoke, letting sink her
    Wings till they trailed in the dust—
In agony sobbed, letting sink her
    Plumes till they trailed in the dust—
    Till they sorrowfully trailed in the dust.

I replied: "This is nothing but dreaming:
    Let us on by this tremulous light!
    Let us bathe in this crystalline light!
Its Sibyllic splendor is beaming
    With Hope and in Beauty tonight:
    See! It flickers up the sky through the night!
Ah, we safely may trust to its gleaming,
    And be sure it will lead us aright—
We surely may trust to a gleaming,
    That cannot but guide us aright,
    Since it flickers up to Heaven through the night."

Thus I pacified Psyche and kissed her,
    And tempted her out of her gloom—
    And conquered her scruples and gloom;
And we passed to the end of the vista,
    But were stopped by the door of a tomb—
    By the door of a legended tomb;
And I said: "What is written, sweet sister,
    On the door of this legended tomb?"
    She replied: "Ulalume—Ulalume!
    'T is the vault of thy lost Ulalume!"

Then my heart it grew ashen and sober
    As the leaves that were crispéd and sere—

As the leaves that were withering and sere;
And I cried: "It was surely October
    On *this* very night of last year
    That I journeyed—I journeyed down here!
    That I brought a dread burden down here—
    On this night of all nights in the year,
    Ah, what demon hath tempted me here?
Well I know, now, this dim lake of Auber—
    This misty mid region of Weir—
Well I know, now, this dank tarn of Auber—
    This ghoul-haunted woodland of Weir."

Said we, then—the two, then: "Ah, can it
    Have been that the woodlandish ghouls—
    The pitiful, the merciful ghouls—
To bar up our way and to ban it
    From the secret that lies in these wolds—
    From the thing that lies hidden in these wolds—
Have drawn up the spectre of a planet
    From the limbo of lunary souls—
This sinfully scintillant planet
    From the Hell of the planetary souls?"

An Enigma

"Seldom we find," says Solomon Don Dunce,
    "Half an idea in the profoundest sonnet.
Through all the flimsy things we see at once
    As easily as through a Naples bonnet—
    Trash of all trash! How *can* a lady don it?
Yet heavier far than your Petrarchan stuff—
Owl-downy nonsense that the faintest puff
    Twirls into trunk-paper the while you con it."
And, veritably, Sol is right enough.
The general tuckermanities are arrant
Bubbles—ephemeral and *so* transparent—
But *this* is, now, you may depend upon it—
Stable, opaque, immortal—all by dint
Of the dear names that lie concealed within 't.

To ———— ———— ————

Not long ago, the writer of these lines,
In the mad pride of intellectuality,
Maintained "the power of words"—denied that ever
A thought arose within the human brain
Beyond the utterance of the human tongue;
And now, as if in mockery of that boast,
Two words—two foreign soft dissyllables—
Italian tones made only to be murmured
By angels dreaming in the moonlit "dew
That hangs like chains of pearl on Hermon hill"—
Have stirred from out the abysses of his heart,
Unthought-like thoughts that are the souls of thought,
Richer, far wilder, far diviner visions
Than even the seraph harper, Israfel,
Who has "the sweetest voice of all God's creatures,"
Could hope to utter. And I! My spells are broken.
The pen falls powerless from my shivering hand.
With thy dear name as text, though bidden by thee,
I cannot write—I cannot speak or think,
Alas, I cannot feel; for 't is not feeling,
This standing motionless upon the golden
Threshold of the wide-open gate of dreams,
Gazing, entranced, adown the gorgeous vista,
And thrilling as I see upon the right,

Upon the left, and all the way along
Amid empurpled vapors, far away
To where the prospect terminates—*thee only.*

TO HELEN

I saw thee once—once only—years ago:
I must not say *how* many—but *not* many.
It was a July midnight; and from out
A full-orbed moon, that, like thine own soul, soaring,
Sought a precipitate pathway up through heaven,
There fell a silvery-silken veil of light,
With quietude, and sultriness, and slumber,
Upon the upturn'd faces of a thousand
Roses that grew in an enchanted garden,
Where no wind dared to stir, unless on tiptoe—
Fell on the upturn'd faces of these roses
That gave out, in return for the love-light,
Their odorous souls in an ecstatic death—
Fell on the upturn'd faces of these roses
That smiled and died in this parterre, enchanted
By thee, and by the poetry of thy presence.

Clad all in white, upon a violet bank
I saw thee half reclining; while the moon
Fell on the upturn'd faces of the roses,
And on thine own, upturn'd—alas, in sorrow!

Was it not Fate that, on this July midnight—
Was it not Fate (whose name is also Sorrow)
That bade me pause before that garden-gate,

To breathe the incense of those slumbering roses?
No footstep stirred: the hated world all slept,
Save only thee and me. (Oh, Heaven! Oh, God!
How my heart beats in coupling those two words!
Save only thee and me). I paused—I looked—
And in an instant all things disappeared.
(Ah, bear in mind this garden was enchanted!)
The pearly lustre of the moon went out:
The mossy banks and the meandering paths,
The happy flowers and the repining trees,
Were seen no more: the very roses' odors
Died in the arms of the adoring airs.
All—all expired save thee—save less than thou:
Save only the divine light in thine eyes—
Save but the soul in thine uplifted eyes.
I saw but them—they were the world to me.
I saw but them—saw only them for hours—
Saw only them until the moon went down.
What wild heart-histories seemed to lie enwritten
Upon those crystalline, celestial spheres!
How dark a wo! Yet how sublime a hope!
How silently serene a sea of pride!
How daring an ambition! Yet how deep—
How fathomless a capacity for love!

But now, at length, dear Dian sank from sight,
Into a western couch of thunder-cloud;
And thou, a ghost, amid the entombing trees
Didst glide away. *Only thine eyes remained.*
They *would not go*—they never yet have gone.
Lighting my lonely pathway home that night,
They have not left me (as my hopes have) since.
They follow me—they lead me through the years.

They are my ministers—yet I their slave.
Their office is to illumine and enkindle—
My duty, *to be saved* by their bright light,
And purified in their electric fire,
And sanctified in their elysian fire.
They fill my soul with Beauty (which is Hope),
And are far up in Heaven—the stars I kneel to
In the sad, silent watches of my night;
While even in the meridian glare of day
I see them still—two sweetly scintillant
Venuses, unextinguished by the sun!

ELDORADO

Gaily bedight
A gallant knight,
In sunshine and in shadow,
Had journeyed long,
Singing a song,
In search of Eldorado.

But he grew old—
This knight so bold—
And o'er his heart a shadow
Fell as he found
No spot of ground
That looked like Eldorado.

And, as his strength
Failed him at length,
He met a pilgrim shadow—
"Shadow," said he,
"Where can it be—
This land of Eldorado?"

"Over the Mountains
Of the Moon,
Down the Valley of the Shadow,
Ride, boldly ride,"
The shade replied,
"If you seek for Eldorado!"

FOR ANNIE

Thank Heaven! The crisis,
    The danger, is past,
And the lingering illness
    Is over at last—
And the fever called "Living"
    Is conquered at last.

Sadly, I know
    I am shorn of my strength,
And no muscle I move
    As I lie at full length—
But no matter! I feel
    I am better at length.

And I rest so composedly,
    Now, in my bed,
That any beholder
    Might fancy me dead—
Might start at beholding me,
    Thinking me dead.

The moaning and groaning,
    The sighing and sobbing,
Are quieted now,
    With that horrible throbbing

At Heart: ah, that horrible,
    Horrible throbbing!

The sickness—the nausea—
    The pitiless pain—
Have ceased, with the fever
    That maddened my brain—
With fever called "Living"
    That burned in my brain.

And oh! Of all tortures
    That torture the worst
Has abated—the terrible
    Torture of thirst
For the naphthaline river
    Of Passion accurst:
I have drank of a water
    That quenches all thirst:

Of a water that flows,
    With a lullaby sound,
From a spring but a very few
    Feet under ground—
From a cavern not very far
    Down under ground.

And ah! Let it never
    Be foolishly said
That my room it is gloomy
    And narrow my bed;
For man never slept
    In a different bed—
And, to *sleep*, you must slumber
    In just such a bed.

My tantalized spirit
    Here blandly reposes,
Forgetting, or never
    Regretting, its roses—
Its old agitations
    Of myrtles and roses:

For now, while so quietly
    Lying, it fancies
A holier odor
    About it, of pansies—
A rosemary odor,
    Commingled with pansies—
With rue and the beautiful
    Puritan pansies.

And so it lies happily,
    Bathing in many
A dream of the truth
    And the beauty of Annie—
Drowned in a bath
    Of the tresses of Annie.

She tenderly kissed me,
    She fondly caressed,
And then I *fell* gently
    To sleep on her breast—
Deeply to sleep
    From the heaven of her breast.

When the light was extinguished,
    She covered me warm,
And she prayed to the angels

To keep me from harm—
To the queen of the angels
To shield me from harm.

And I lie so composedly,
Now, in my bed
(Knowing her love),
That you fancy me dead—
And I rest so contentedly,
Now, in my bed
(With her love at my breast),
That you fancy me dead—
That you shudder to look at me,
Thinking me dead:

But my heart it is brighter
Than all of the many
Stars of the heaven,
For it sparkles with Annie—
It glows with the fire
Of the love of my Annie—
With the thought of the light
Of the eyes of my Annie.

SONNET—TO MY MOTHER

Because I feel that, in the Heavens above,
    The angels, whispering to one another,
Can find, among their burning terms of love,
    None so devotional as that of "Mother,"
Therefore by that sweet name I long have called you—
    You who are more than mother unto me,
And fill my heart of hearts, where Death installed you
    In setting my Virginia's spirit free.
My mother—my own mother, who died early,
    Was but the mother of myself; but you
Are mother to the one I loved so dearly,
    And thus are dearer than the mother I knew
By that infinity with which my wife
    Was dearer to my soul than its soul-life.

ANNABEL LEE

It was many and many a year ago,
    In a kingdom by the sea,
That a maiden there lived whom you may know
    By the name of Annabel Lee;
And this maiden she lived with no other thought
    Than to love and be loved by me.

She was a child and *I* was a child,
    In this kingdom by the sea,
But we loved with a love that was more than love—
    I and my Annabel Lee—
With a love that the winged seraphs of Heaven
    Coveted her and me.

And this was the reason that, long ago,
    In this kingdom by the sea,
A wind blew out of a cloud by night
    Chilling my Annabel Lee;
So that her highborn kinsmen came
    And bore her away from me,
To shut her up in a sepulchre
    In this kingdom by the sea.

The angels, not half so happy in Heaven,
    Went envying her and me:

Yes! That was the reason (as all men know,
    In this kingdom by the sea)
That the wind came out of a cloud, chilling
    And killing my Annabel Lee.
But our love it was stronger by far than the love
    Of those who were older than we—
    Of many far wiser than we—
And neither the angels in Heaven above
    Nor the demons down under the sea,
Can ever dissever my soul from the soul
    Of the beautiful Annabel Lee:

For the moon never beams without bringing me dreams
    Of the beautiful Annabel Lee;
And the stars never rise but I see the bright eyes
    Of the beautiful Annabel Lee;
And so, all the night-tide, I lie down by the side
Of my darling, my darling, my life and my bride,
    In her sepulchre there by the sea—
    In her tomb by the side of the sea.

THE BELLS

I

Hear the sledges with the bells—
Silver bells!
What a world of merriment their melody foretells!
How they tinkle, tinkle, tinkle,
In the icy air of night!
While the stars that oversprinkle
All the heavens, seem to twinkle
With a crystalline delight;
Keeping time, time, time,
In a sort of Runic rhyme,
To the tintinnabulation that so musically wells
From the bells, bells, bells, bells,
Bells, bells, bells—
From the jingling and the tinkling of the bells.

II

Hear the mellow wedding bells—
Golden bells!
What a world of happiness their harmony foretells!
Through the balmy air of night
How they ring out their delight!
From the molten-golden notes,
And all in tune,
What a liquid ditty floats

To the turtle-dove that listens, while she gloats
On the moon!
Oh, from out the sounding cells,
What a gush of euphony voluminously wells!
How it swells!
How it dwells
On the Future! How it tells
Of the rapture that impels
To the swinging and the ringing
Of the bells, bells, bells—
Of the bells, bells, bells, bells,
Bells, bells, bells—
To the rhyming and the chiming of the bells!

III

Hear the loud alarum bells—
Brazen bells!
What a tale of terror, now, their turbulency tells!
In the startled ear of night
How they scream out their affright!
Too much horrified to speak,
They can only shriek, shriek,
Out of tune,
In a clamorous appealing to the mercy of the fire,
In a mad expostulation with the deaf and frantic fire,
Leaping higher, higher, higher,
With a desperate desire,
And a resolute endeavor
Now—now to sit, or never,
By the side of the pale-faced moon.
Oh, the bells, bells, bells!
What a tale their terror tells
Of Despair!

How they clang, and clash, and roar!
What a horror they outpour
On the bosom of the palpitating air!
Yet the ear, it fully knows,
By the twanging
And the clanging,
How the danger ebbs and flows;
Yet the ear distinctly tells,
In the jangling
And the wrangling,
How the danger sinks and swells,
By the sinking or the swelling in the anger of the bells—
Of the bells,
Of the bells, bells, bells, bells,
Bells, bells, bells—
In the clamour and the clangor of the bells!

IV

Hear the tolling of the bells—
Iron bells!
What a world of solemn thought their monody compels!
In the silence of the night,
How we shiver with affright
At the melancholy menace of their tone!
For every sound that floats
From the rust within their throats
Is a groan.
And the people—ah, the people—
They that dwell up in the steeple,
All alone,
And who tolling, tolling, tolling,
In that muffled monotone,
Feel a glory in so rolling

On the human heart a stone—
They are neither man nor woman—
They are neither brute nor human—
They are Ghouls:
And their king it is who tolls:
And he rolls, rolls, rolls,
Rolls
A pæan from the bells!
And his merry bosom swells
With the pæan of the bells!
And he dances, and he yells;
Keeping time, time, time,
In a sort of Runic rhyme,
To the pæan of the bells—
Of the bells:
Keeping time, time, time,
In a sort of Runic rhyme,
To the throbbing of the bells—
Of the bells, bells, bells—
To the sobbing of the bells;
Keeping time, time, time,
As he knells, knells, knells,
In a happy Runic rhyme,
To the rolling of the bells—
Of the bells, bells, bells:
To the tolling of the bells—
Of the bells, bells, bells, bells,
Bells, bells, bells—
To the moaning and the groaning of the bells.

ELIZABETH

Elizabeth, it surely is most fit
[Logic and common usage so commanding]
In thy own book that first thy name be writ,
Zeno and other sages notwithstanding;
And *I* have other reasons for so doing
Besides my innate love of contradiction;
Each poet—*if* a poet—in pursuing
The muses thro' their bowers of Truth or Fiction,
Has studied very little of his part,
Read nothing, written less—in short's a fool
Endued with neither soul, nor sense, nor art,
Being ignorant of one important rule,
Employed in even the theses of the school—
Called—I forget the heathenish Greek name—
[Called anything, its meaning is the same]
"Always write *first* things uppermost in the heart."

SERENADE

So sweet the hour, so calm the time,
I feel it more than half a crime,
When Nature sleeps and stars are mute,
To mar the silence ev'n with lute.
At rest on ocean's brilliant dyes
An image of Elysium lies:
Seven Pleiades entranced in Heaven,
Form in the deep another seven:
Endymion nodding from above
Sees in the sea a second love.
Within the valleys dim and brown,
And on the spectral mountain's crown,
The wearied light is dying down,
And earth, and stars, and sea, and sky
Are redolent of sleep, as I
Am redolent of thee and thine
Enthralling love, my Adeline.
But list, O list, so soft and low
Thy lover's voice tonight shall flow,
That, scarce awake, thy soul shall deem
My words the music of a dream.
Thus, while no single sound too rude
Upon thy slumber shall intrude,
Our thoughts, our souls—O God above!
In every deed shall mingle, love.

INDEX OF FIRST LINES

SUGGESTED READING

BUDD, LOUIS J., AND EDWIN HARRISON CADY, EDS. *On Poe.* Durham, NC: Duke University Press, 1993.

HAYES, KEVIN J., ED. *The Cambridge Companion to Edgar Allan Poe.* New York: Cambridge University Press, 2002.

———. *Poe and the Printed Word.* New York: Cambridge University Press, 2000.

HOFFMAN, DANIEL. *Poe Poe Poe Poe Poe Poe Poe.* 1972. Reprinted. Baton Rouge: Louisiana State University Press, 1998.

HUTCHISSON, JAMES M. *Poe.* Jackson: University Press of Mississippi, 2005.

LEVIN, HARRY. *The Power of Blackness: Hawthorne, Poe, Melville.* 1958. Reprinted. Athens: Ohio University Press, 1980.

PARKS, EDD WINFIELD. *Edgar Allan Poe as Literary Critic.* Athens: University of Georgia Press, 1964.

QUINN, ARTHUR HOBSON. *Edgar Allan Poe: A Critical Biography.* 1941. Reprinted. Baltimore: Johns Hopkins University Press, 1998.

QUINN, PATRICK F. *The French Face of Edgar Poe.* 1957. Carbondale: Southern Illinois University Press, 1971.

SILVERMAN, KENNETH. *Edgar A. Poe: Mournful and Never-ending Remembrance.* New York: HarperCollins, 1991.

VINES, LOIS, ED. *Poe Abroad: Influence, Reputation, Affinities.* Iowa City: University of Iowa Press, 1999.

WALSH, JOHN EVANGELIST. *Midnight Dreary: The Mysterious Death of Edgar Allan Poe.* New Brunswick, NJ: Rutgers University Press, 1998.

ZIMMERMAN, BRETT. *Edgar Allan Poe: Rhetoric and Style.* Montreal: McGill-Queen's University Press, 2005.